the
Academy
in
Transition

General Education and the Assessment Reform Agenda

by Peter Ewell

Published by the
Association of American Colleges and Universities
1818 R Street, NW, Washington, DC 20009
www.aacu.org
Copyright © 2004
ISBN 0-911696-99-7
Cover photos: University of Portland and Franklin College

Contents

the Academy in Transition

To order additional copies of this publication or to find out about other AAC&U publications, visit www.aacu.org, e-mail pub_desk@aacu.org, or call 202.387.3760.

About This Series

The Association of American Colleges and Universities (AAC&U) has a long history of working with college leaders across the country to articulate the aims of a liberal education in our time. AAC&U is distinctive as a higher education association. Its mission focuses centrally on the quality of student learning and the changing purpose and nature of undergraduate curricula.

AAC&U has taken the lead in encouraging and facilitating dialogue on issues of importance to the higher education community for many years. Through a series of publications called The Academy in Transition—launched in 1998 with the much-acclaimed *Contemporary Understandings of Liberal Education*—AAC&U has helped fuel dialogue on such issues as the globalization of the undergraduate curricula, the growth of interdisciplinary studies, how liberal education has changed historically, and the increase of college-level learning in high school. The purpose of the series—now including nine titles—is to analyze changes taking place in key areas of undergraduate education and to provide "road maps" illustrating the directions and destinations of the changing academy.

During transitions, it is important to understand context and history and to retain central values, even as forms and structures that have supported those values may have to be adapted to new circumstances. For instance, AAC&U is convinced that a practical and engaged liberal education is a sound vision for the new academy, even if the meanings and practices of liberal education are in the process of being altered by changing conditions. As the titles in this series suggest, AAC&U's vision encompasses a high-quality liberal education for all students that emphasizes connections between academic disciplines and practical and theoretical knowledge, prizes general education as central to an educated person, and includes global and cross-cultural knowledge and perspectives. Collectively, these essays point to a more purposeful, robust, and efficient academy that is now in the process of being created. They also encourage thoughtful, historically informed dialogue about the future of the academy.

AAC&U encourages faculty members, academic leaders, and all those who care about the future of our colleges and universities to use these papers as a point of departure for their own analyses of the directions of educational change. We hope these essays will encourage academics to think broadly and creatively about the educational communities we inherit, and, by our contributions, the educational communities we want to create.

Debra Humphreys
Vice President for Communications and Public Affairs
Association of American Colleges and Universities

I. Introduction:

The Examined Life

It has been nearly twenty years since *Integrity in the College Curriculum* (AAC 1985) called for a new vision of liberal education. *Greater Expectations: A New Vision for Learning as a Nation Goes to College* (2002), a recent report from the Association of American Colleges and Universities, appropriately renews this call for the twenty-first century, but as we look ahead, those of us involved in assessment reform need to remember that we have been at this business for almost a generation now. Although we have some small victories to show for our work, we have hardly achieved the large-scale transformation of teaching and learning we once envisioned.

Our vision has always demanded three things that, like the components of liberal education itself, are intertwined and inseparable:

1. A clearly articulated, collective, and detailed vision of the attributes and abilities of an educated person
2. Coherence and connectedness in the educational experiences that are intended to yield these ends
3. Defensible evidence of their accomplishment

Others have said similar things—most notably, the members of the Study Group on the Conditions of Excellence in Higher Education who authored *Involvement in Learning* in 1984 (NIE). Unfortunately, many more disagreed with these arguments, or simply ignored them, and institutions did little to systematically change their instructional practices. The reasons are not hard to see. Change was hard and the need for it unclear. More importantly, perhaps, in the press for implementation we lost the integration that made the original vision so compelling. Parts of the agenda were implemented in some places—comprehensive assessment, active learning strategies, or service learning and learning communities—but not in the coherent fashion that was intended.

Today, the higher education community is at a particularly important crossroads in this conversation because of the intersection of two opposing forces that are increasingly

> *Although we have some small victories to show for our work, we have hardly achieved the large-scale transformation of teaching and learning we once envisioned.*

shaping our actions. The "bad news" is that a particular—and forceful—ideology of assessment linked to accountability is being advanced in Washington and elsewhere as a recipe for "fixing" education at all levels. This ideology, of course, presents an "examined life" that is emphatically not worth living, but we ignore it at our peril. The "good news" is that we are finally developing confidence in approaches that are capable of making scholarly evidence of student academic achievement beyond grades both credible and academically acceptable. But in the light of the bad news we have little time to lose in pressing to make this vision a reality. With appropriate emphasis on the good news, in the following pages I want to examine the conjunction of these two forces in the particular context of general education.

How We Got Here

Let me begin with the external forces—the "bad news" story—because understanding how we got here is critical to understanding how we can move forward. And, in fact, the account of how we got here is complicated and contains some important cautionary tales.
When the national assessment movement began in the mid-1980s, those of us who were involved with it shared some implicit beliefs about assessment's potential to transform teaching and learning. Most importantly, we believed that

- a focus on learning outcomes would lead faculty and institutional leaders to rethink—and ultimately restructure—curricula and pedagogy;
- evidence-based inquiry about teaching and learning would be construed as responsible scholarship—faculty would want to engage in it and institutions would welcome the chance to get beyond "management by anecdote";
- the results of such inquiry would be used for continuous improvement and the resulting "feedback loop" would spur iterative and ongoing institutional learning;
- "assessment" as a technique would only have meaning in the context of a larger process of institutional metamorphosis that would involve establishing high expectations for students, promoting engaging pedagogies, and transforming faculty work.

These core beliefs were implicit in many of the early writings about assessment (e.g., AAHE 1992). In retrospect, they seem pretty naive. Many (if not most) institutions were captured by a model of assessment that was excessively mechanical and process-centered—one that did *not* embody the kind of ongoing institutional learning that we hoped would develop.

One reason for this was that, through too early emphasis on technique, we let assessment get excessively distanced from the day-to-day business of teaching and learning. Not seeing the connection—and rightly fearing an awful lot of work—many faculty started avoiding the topic entirely. At the same time, assessment became something that external bodies—state governments and accreditation organizations—forcefully asked institutions to do. The fact that an activity that was not seen by faculty as intrinsically important seemed only to be done at the behest of somebody else exacerbated the first tendency. Assessment increasingly became the "A-word"—an *add-on* to teaching and learning, rather than something integrally related to it, and the province of bureaucrats and bean counters.

The fact that so many institutions failed to seriously engage assessment under these conditions is perhaps understandable. But it has resulted in a serious shortfall in our current ability to answer legitimate public questions about results. And into this vacuum has come a powerful contrasting ideology—embodied in such initiatives as the federal No Child Left Behind (NCLB) Act—that proposes to answer these questions in a different way.

While it seems clear that this ideology will not completely dominate conversations about the Higher Education Act Reauthorization in the near future, it does represent a politically popular approach that also characterizes the policy attitudes of the majority of state and federal lawmakers. For this reason, it requires a serious response from higher education. And there are particular features of the policy approach embodied in NCLB that make it so politically compelling—features that we will have to do our best to match in any alternative we advance.

We need to reaffirm the values we started with twenty years ago — before assessment became the A-word.

First, NCLB sets clear and visible standards of academic achievement. Though we may not like an approach that is based almost entirely on external, standardized tests (and in fact such an approach is highly unlikely at this point for higher education), our alternatives must be equally public about our expectations for learning and the extent to which we have achieved them.

Second, it is consequential about performance. Schools that do not perform well face substantial negative consequences as a result—a form of accountability that, like hanging, surely focuses the mind. Our alternatives, while hopefully neither draconian nor negative, need to be crafted in such a way that they recognize publicly cases in which achievement may have fallen short, and are clear about what actions will be taken in response.

Third, it is deliberately comparative—driven by a single commensurable yardstick of performance to which all are held accountable. While we may in some ways legitimately object that the missions of colleges and universities differ, and that the resulting diversity is a significant strength of higher education in America, our alternatives need also to be able to respond to charges that we are simply using our variety to duck the fact that there are certain levels and types of attainment that ought to characterize the recipients of every baccalaureate degree.

Matching these compelling aspects of NCLB in an alternative approach to assessment in general education will naturally be a tall order. But we can start by building on the framework provided by the *Greater Expectations* report and on the techniques that have already been developed on some campuses. We need to reaffirm the values we started with twenty years ago—before assessment became the A-word—in the light of this growing experience, these new techniques, and the rising legitimacy of the scholarship of teaching and learning.

Drawing on the architecture of *Greater Expectations*, this paper reflects on how we can link assessment and general education. My reflections are organized around not one but four A-words: Abilities, Alignment, Assessment, and Action. I contend that knitting these four together yields a final "A"—Accountability—*not* in the narrow sense of No Child Left Behind, but in the original professional sense of assuming genuine collective responsibility for the academy and its integrity.

II. Abilities

I will begin with Abilities, by which I mean the clear specification of what a student ought to know and be able to do as well as the qualities of educational intentionality and connectedness that we want her or him to embody as a result of general education. Let me offer two initial observations here.

First, in an admirable attempt to be comprehensive about what it means to be an "educated person," we tend to name an awful lot of abilities. There are, for instance, some twenty-one separate abilities named in *Greater Expectations*, all of them necessary and noble. But from the perspective of public communication, we need to single out a few of them—communications, the ability to work well in diverse groups, or quantitative and information literacy, for example—as our primary common assessment agenda for general education. This strategy could crystallize public opinion and mobilize action, as the National Education Goals Panel did some fifteen years ago when it called upon the nation's colleges to graduate students who could "think critically, communicate effectively, and solve problems" (1991, 237).

Second, it is often claimed that the ends of general education embodied in these named abilities are excruciatingly difficult to describe and assess—and are quite different from the outcomes of specialized knowledge or training. Admittedly, we are talking about an incredible range of things, some of which appear at first glance ineffable. *Greater Expectations*, for example, lists a set of "intellectual and practical skills" that range from the relatively straightforward—communication and problem solving—to far more complex abilities like "intellectual agility and managing change" (AAC&U 2002, 15). At the same time, it embraces personal qualities like intellectual honesty, active civic participation, and self-understanding. But there is a compelling case for not seeing these abilities as limited to a "generally educated" person. They are also aspects of personal and professional mastery, as described in the marvelous literature on the differences between novice and expert practice (for a summary, see Bransford, Brown, and Cocking 1999, ch. 2).

What this suggests is quite simple: the assessment of general education is about examining the consequences not of any particular body of coursework that may be labeled as

> *The assessment of general education must be integrally linked to the major.*

"general education" but of the undergraduate experience as a whole. This conclusion has a real implication for practice. It's not enough to examine general education in the class-based settings of core or distribution requirements, however embedded and authentic these assessments may be. We must also examine how these abilities infuse and inform expert practice. The assessment of general education, in short, must be integrally linked to the major.

In the same vein, I have learned two additional lessons about the slippery matter of articulating abilities. First, it's more useful to start with the *actual practice* of the ability than with the stated outcome. Phrases like "intellectual agility" have great charm, but mean little in the absence of an actual student performance that might demonstrate them.

The performance that the student exhibits on the assessment is the definition of the ability itself.

To construct assessment techniques, formal assessment design, as described in the textbooks, demands ever more detailed verbal specifications of the outcomes or competencies to be developed. But it is often more helpful to go the other way. Given a broad general descriptor like "intellectual agility," can you imagine a *very concrete* situation in which somebody might display this ability, and how they might actually behave? Better still, can you quickly specify the parameters of an *assignment* or *problem* that might demand a particular level of this ability for success? The performance that the student exhibits on the assessment is the definition of the ability itself; the ability has no independent existence.

Starting with the concrete in this manner can also quickly uncover lurking inconsistencies in the way we think about a given ability that might later lead to trouble. Nowhere has this been more apparent than in our communications with external stakeholders. For example, business leaders and academics will quickly concur that all graduates ought to have attributes like "critical thinking," but when you describe the ability in action—what its exercise looks like in a real situation—they may have quite different views about what it actually means. Academics tend to anchor the ability in a student's capacity to recognize flaws in reasoning, examine evidence, and compare two lines of argument. Business people, by contrast, tend to emphasize performance in ill-structured situations—finding the "problem to solve," for example, and knowing how to work around missing information or when to stop after identifying a "good enough" solution. These are quite different abilities masquerading under a common name.

From an accountability standpoint, the implication is clear. Rather than saying simply that our graduates achieve at "level 4" in critical thinking (or some such ability), we need to succinctly describe exactly what they were asked to do and how well they performed. A good illustration of this is the way the National Adult Literacy Survey was constructed some fifteen years ago. Its designers did not start with abstract abilities and then try to build an assessment to determine if people had them. They instead began with a set of concrete tasks that citizens ought to be able to perform, like reading a bus schedule or interpreting a graph, that any external observer could instantly see were important. By doing so, they essentially proclaimed, "we hold these tasks to be self-evident." This strategy worked very well for public communication. And, as I will describe later, it has clear implications for the kinds of assessments we construct.

III. Alignment

Too often curricular structure or pedagogy is not meaningfully aligned with our statements of desired outcomes for general education, however they are defined. In fact, on many campuses, statements of intended outcomes for general education were invented primarily to guide *assessment*, not teaching and learning practice. This curious condition, of course, is in part a result of assessment being done at the behest of others. Accreditation agencies require "assessment," and this appears predicated on the development of outcomes statements. But there are few accreditation requirements as yet that look at how well such statements, once they are established, are connected to pedagogy or curricular design. (As the recent AAC&U publication *Taking Responsibility for the Quality of the Baccalaureate Degree* [2004] demonstrates, some accreditors have recognized this problem and are beginning to fix it.)

The popular move toward more embedded forms of assessment in general education is also beginning to address this issue by forcing institutions to "map" the places where particular abilities are taught—and, therefore, where they might be assessed already—in a more explicit way than before. And this exercise also starts to address a major gap in our knowledge about most general education curricula: the fact that we do not know exactly how they are working. This is not the same thing as knowing how well they are fostering desired abilities. Instead, it poses a more basic question about the extent to which the students' experience of the curriculum is consistent with the "design for learning" originally intended by the faculty. Faculty are generally great designers when it comes to general education, and some curricular schemes are masterpieces of complexity. But there is often very little information available about how students are making course choices and what the consequences of those choices are. Studies along these lines can be extremely fruitful in general education. Moreover, the problem of how students choose courses is now complicated by the growing incidence of "multiple pathways" students.

> *Taking alignment seriously has implications for how things are taught, not just for curricular structure and content.*

9

A first point of advice here is to sort out the many purposes of what we call general education and the specific roles that particular learning experiences are intended to play. I note four of these purposes here:

1. Development of prerequisite skills needed for later work (e.g., in communication or in math)

2. Development of abilities that cut across disciplines, like critical thinking or problem solving

3. Development of general knowledge about particular disciplines and experience with different modes of inquiry

4. Collegiate socialization—learning how to "do college" by learning how to use a library (or the Web), or how to plan and carry out an independent intellectual project

Distinctions among these various purposes ought to dictate where in the curriculum particular learning experiences are located and when students engage in them.

We know, however, that students do not always follow our prescriptions. They may choose to postpone or avoid math or writing, for example, or simply take as many classes as possible that fit their personal schedules. Analyses of how students "act out" general education also frequently reveal an astounding lack of coherence because courses taken sequentially often are not connected to one another. Consequently, there is often a lot of "re-work" needed—faculty are forced to address topics in a subsequent course that they presumed students had learned in a prerequisite. Such analyses may also reveal that a particular course is not doing the job assigned to it in the curriculum for one reason or another.

Finally, taking alignment seriously has implications for *how* things are taught, not just for curricular structure and content. I learned an early lesson on this from an attempt at the College of William and Mary to assess critical thinking through a systematic cross section of student writing in courses that required it. Faculty there found that they simply couldn't evaluate critical thinking in a majority of cases because the assignments generating the student writing didn't ask for it. Such systematic sampling of student work can help us determine if we are actually teaching the abilities that we hope we are. For instance, Truman State University recently used this technique to look for spontaneous interdisciplinary connections in student work. Examples of this kind call attention to the fact that assessment in general education should address issues of alignment explicitly and directly by generating evidence of student behavior, not just by examining outcomes.

IV. Assessment

The third anticipated A-word, Assessment, remains resolutely focused on outcomes—the extent to which abilities are attained. Rather than discussing specific assessment techniques, I want to confine my reflections here to some major choices in design and approach, and to how these choices may be particularly conditioned by the need to provide credible evidence of student academic achievement for external constituencies.

To begin with, it is useful to distinguish two quite different overall approaches, which we can name after two predominant animal body types: "exoskeletal" and "endoskeletal." *Both* approaches may be helpful for developing effective assessment in the context of general education.

The exoskeletal approach is probably the most easily explained, as it resembles the classic early picture of assessment that most campuses adopted in the mid-1980s—usually in response to a state mandate or emerging accreditation requirements. Under this approach, assessment opportunities are created *outside* and *alongside* the regular curriculum. They are intended to be special and infrequent occasions when student learning, usually in the aggregate, can be examined with greater deliberation and precision than in the classroom or through standard grading. Indeed, it was precisely because grades had become suspect as indicators of student learning that this more "scientific" alternative was evolved twenty years ago. Its early manifestation in general education settings tended to center on externally obtained examinations and

The exoskeletal approach resembles the classic early picture of assessment that most campuses adopted in the mid-1980s — usually in response to a state mandate or emerging accreditation requirements.

"Assessment Days." But more authentic versions now center on techniques like sophomore writing exercises and portfolios. These newer approaches are far more compelling and faculty-centered than those that only have students take the Academic Profile or the ACT Collegiate Assessment of Academic Proficiency (ACT-CAAP), but they still stand outside the regular day-to-day process of teaching and learning.

Several respected and venerable curricular designs in general education employed an exoskeletal approach to student assessment. One classic was the Core at the University of Chicago in the 1930s, which featured general examinations—developed by Benjamin Bloom of "Bloom's Taxonomy," among others—in various fields. Also instructive is the experience of many small liberal arts colleges which, through the 1950s, administered the now-defunct Education Testing Service (ETS) Area Exams to all students and required a culminating piece of scholarship in the major. It is important to stress that although these testing occasions occurred in addition to classes, they were considered an integral part of the design for general education. Students expected them, and performance on them was consequential. There is a lot of wisdom in these historic approaches.

The endoskeletal approach to assessment has evolved more recently, largely in an attempt to avoid the worst consequences of the "add-on" mentality. Here, the attempt is to embed occasions for assessment seamlessly throughout a given student's learning experience as she or he progresses. Under one version of this approach, specific assignments that explicitly address particular abil-

The endoskeletal approach to assessment has evolved largely in an attempt to avoid the worst consequences of the "add-on" mentality.

ities are strategically laced throughout general education coursework and are intended to do double duty. On one level, these assignments are a regular expectation of students and are graded as such. However, the standards and methods used to examine the resulting work are keyed not just to what the individual faculty member expects, but also to a collectively agreed-upon set of rubrics or grading guides that both align faculty judgments and enable the institution to determine aggregate patterns of strength and weakness with respect to the ability in question. Other versions of this approach relax the constraint of common rubric-based grading by allowing faculty to grade in their own way for the record, scoring only a sample of student work at a later point to garner assessment information. Writing is the ability most frequently examined in this way. The advantage here, of course, is that assessment activity is much closer to the business at hand and is entirely transparent to students. And creating the design in the first place helps ensure curricular coherence. The challenge is to round up all these judgments and be consistent.

Like all metaphors, the skeletal one is imperfect, and there are many sound "intermediate forms" in between. The point is simply to be quite deliberate about deciding questions of assessment as an integral part of curricular design. This can be illustrated with two examples drawn from quite different institutions with which I have worked—one a major public research university and one a well-known liberal arts college. Both are in the process of developing a new approach to general education and so have the opportunity to engineer assessment into their designs from the outset. And both are aware of the need for the results of any

institutional leaders to act individually on their own campuses, and to act in concert to support the development of credible and public aggregate assessments of collegiate learning. In the current climate of political divisiveness and funding shortfalls, this will admittedly not be easy. But not to act is to risk the very existence of an academy that, a generation ago, most of us were proud to have joined.

Works Cited

American Association for Higher Education (AAHE). 1992. *Principles of good practice for assessing student learning.* Washington, DC: American Association for Higher Education.

Association of American Colleges (AAC). 1985. *Integrity in the college curriculum: A report to the academic community.* Washington, DC: Association of American Colleges.

Association of American Colleges and Universities (AAC&U). 2002. *Greater expectations: A new vision for learning as a nation goes to college.* Washington, DC: Association of American Colleges and Universities.

. 2004. *Taking responsibility for the quality of the baccalaureate degree: A report from the Greater Expectations project on accreditation and assessment.* Washington, DC: Association of American Colleges and Universities.

Bransford, J. D., A. L. Brown, and R. R. Cocking. 1999. *How people learn: Brain, mind, experience, and school.* Washington, DC: National Academy Press.

National Education Goals Panel. 1991. *The 1991 national education goals report.* Washington, DC: National Education Goals Panel.

National Institute for Education (NIE). 1984. *Involvement in learning: Report of the study group on the conditions of excellence in American higher education.* Washington, DC: U.S. Government Printing Office.

Western Association of Schools and Colleges. 2001. *Handbook of accreditation.* Oakland, CA: Western Association of Schools and Colleges, Senior Commission.

AAC&U Statement on Liberal Learning

A truly liberal education is one that prepares us to live responsible, productive, and creative lives in a dramatically changing world. It is an education that fosters a well-grounded intellectual resilience, a disposition toward lifelong learning, and an acceptance of responsibility for the ethical consequences of our ideas and actions. Liberal education requires that we understand the foundations of knowledge and inquiry about nature, culture and society; that we master core skills of perception, analysis, and expression; that we cultivate a respect for truth; that we recognize the importance of historical and cultural context; and that we explore connections among formal learning, citizenship, and service to our communities.

We experience the benefits of liberal learning by pursuing intellectual work that is honest, challenging, and significant, and by preparing ourselves to use knowledge and power in responsible ways. Liberal learning is not confined to particular fields of study. What matters in liberal education is substantial content, rigorous methodology and an active engagement with the societal, ethical, and practical implications of our learning. The spirit and value of liberal learning are equally relevant to all forms of higher education and to all students.

Because liberal learning aims to free us from the constraints of ignorance, sectarianism, and myopia, it prizes curiosity and seeks to expand the boundaries of human knowledge. By its nature, therefore, liberal learning is global and pluralistic. It embraces the diversity of ideas and experiences that characterize the social, natural, and intellectual world. To acknowledge such diversity in all its forms is both an intellectual commitment and a social responsibility, for nothing less will equip us to understand our world and to pursue fruitful lives. The ability to think, to learn, and to express oneself both rigorously and creatively, the capacity to understand ideas and issues in context, the commitment to live in society, and the yearning for truth are fundamental features of our humanity. In centering education upon these qualities, liberal learning is society's best investment in our shared future.

Adopted by the Board of Directors of the Association of American Colleges & Universities, October 1998